MY OWN BOOK OF COLOURS

ISBN 13: 978-1-964243-57-3
ISBN 10: 1-964243-57-3

Permission request(s) should be submitted to the publisher in writing at one of the addresses below:
CHEETAH® Toys & More, LLC
207 Main Street, 3rd Floor
Hartford, CT 06106 USA

Port Antonio PO
Portland, Jamaica

info@mycheetahinc.com
paulettetrowers@yahoo.com
WhatsApp: 860-781-1726
876-909-6311

MY OWN BOOK OF COLOURS

MY OWN BOOK OF COLOURS

MY OWN BOOK OF
COLOURS

Black

White

2

Grey

Blue

Brown

Green

Indigo

7

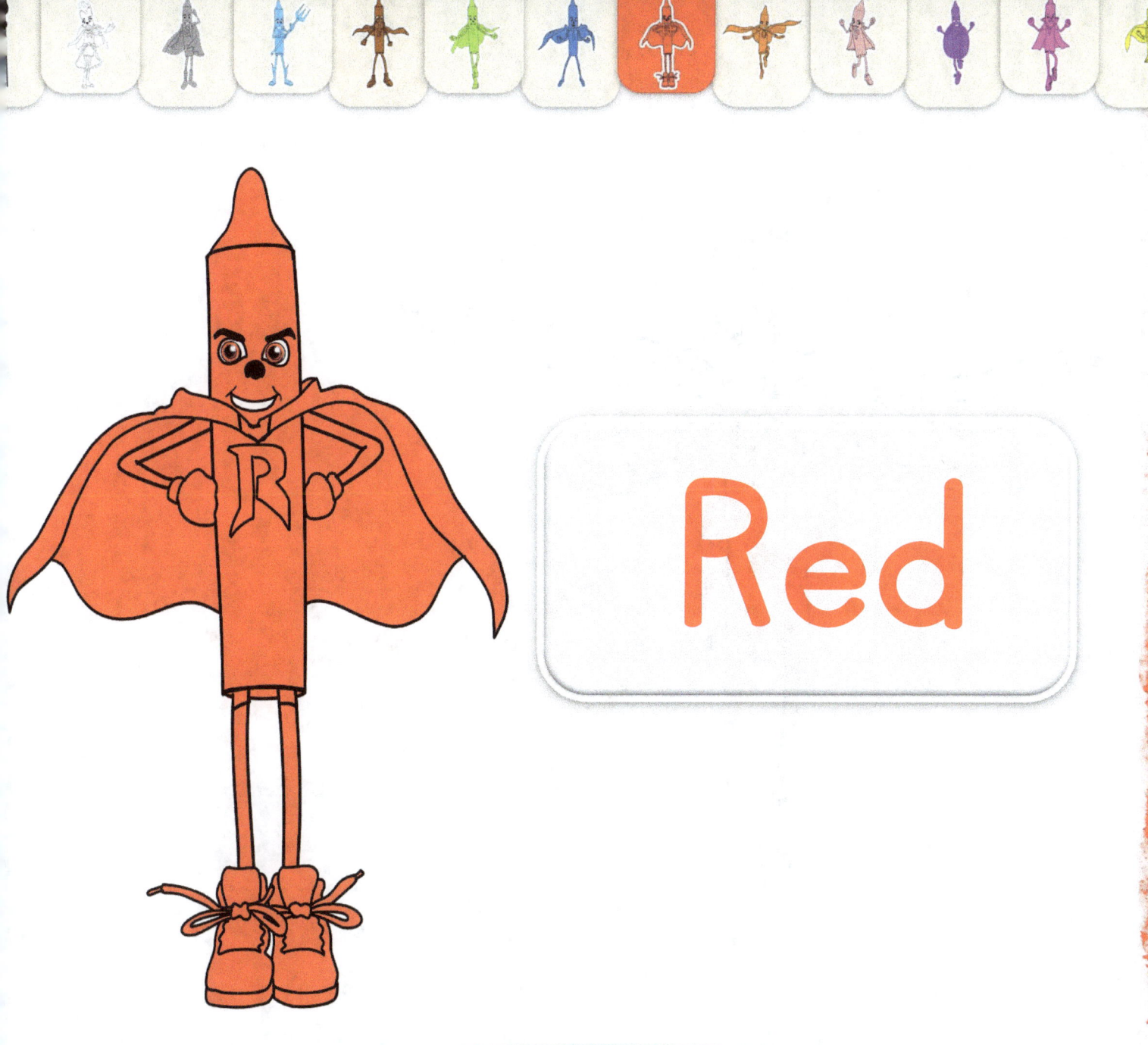

Red

Orange

Pink

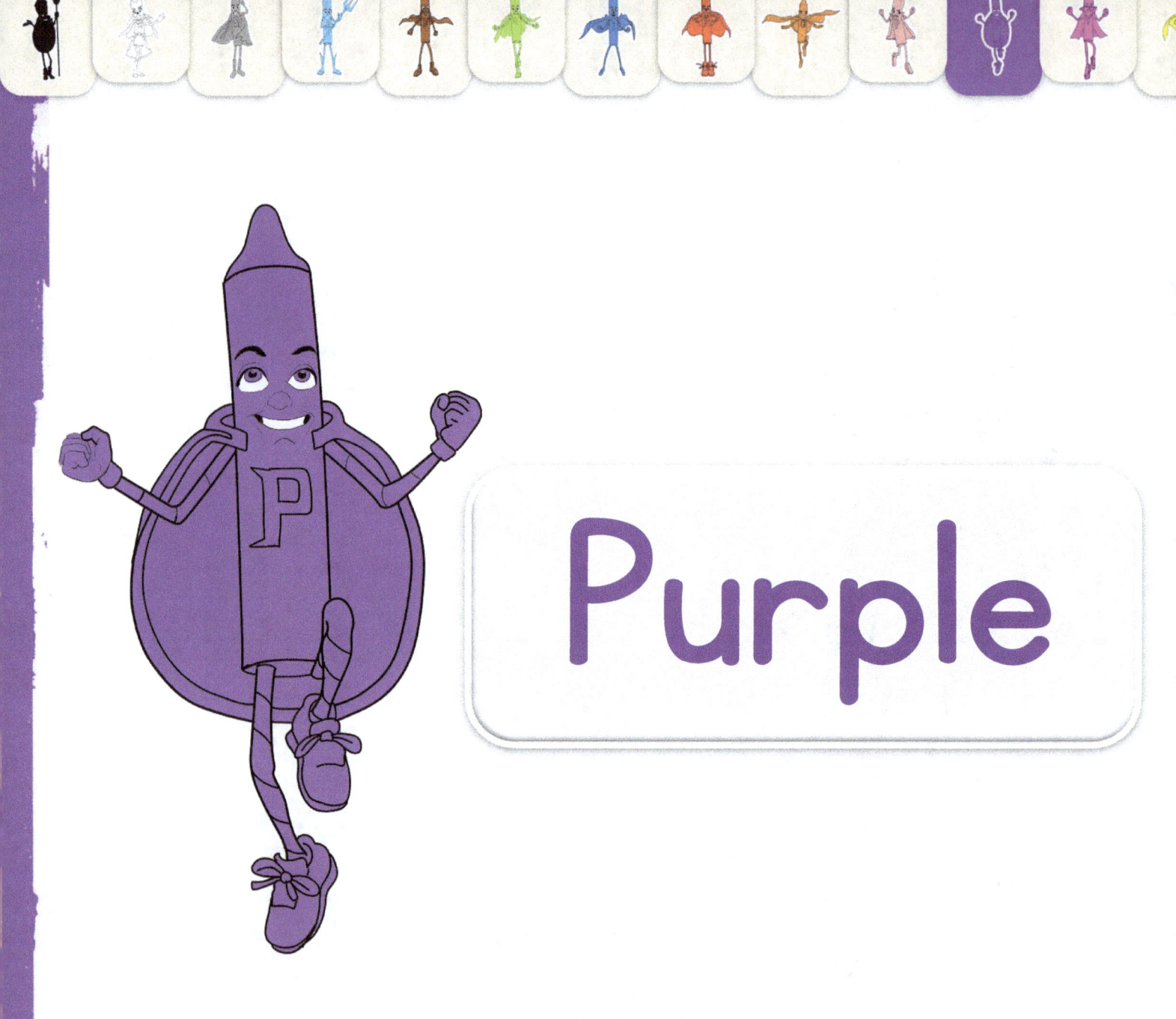

Purple

Violet

Yellow

13